Introduction

Introduction
Context and Importance of the 2016 Election.

The 2016 US presidential election was a watershed moment in American political history, with extraordinary occurrences, profound societal divisions, and a substantial shift in the political landscape. The election witnessed the growth of unusual candidates, the power of social media, and greater scrutiny of the political process. Understanding the background and significance of this election necessitates a review of the political atmosphere before the election, an introduction to the important candidates, and an examination of the event's significance in American history.

Overview of the Political Climate Prior to the Election

The United States underwent dramatic transformation and turmoil in the years preceding the 2016 presidential election. The country was emerging from the Great Recession, and while the economy had recovered, many Americans continued to suffer the consequences of economic hardship. Income inequality, job instability, and growing healthcare costs were top concerns among the general population.

Politically, the country was extremely divided. The two major parties, Democrats and Republicans, were increasingly split on critical topics like as immigration, healthcare, and foreign policy. The Obama administration, which had served two terms, received criticism from both sides of the aisle. Conservatives opposed Obama's policies on healthcare (particularly the Affordable Care Act), immigration, and environmental restrictions, whilst progressives were dissatisfied with what they perceived as inadequate progress on problems such as economic inequality and criminal justice reform.

Social concerns had an important part in determining the political environment. The Black Lives Matter movement raised awareness about systematic racism and police violence, sparking worldwide protests and calls for reform. The Supreme Court's decision to allow same-sex marriage nationally in 2015 was a watershed moment for LGBTQ+ rights, but it also fueled cultural and political conflicts.

The growth of populism throughout the world, as highlighted by movements like Brexit in the United Kingdom, reflected rising discontent with established political institutions and elites. This anger was echoed in the United States, paving the way for an election that challenged traditional political conventions.

Introduction to Key Candidates: Hillary Clinton and Donald Trump

The 2016 presidential election featured two of the most divisive and well-known candidates in contemporary American history: Hillary Clinton and Donald Trump.

Hillary Clinton began the campaign as the Democratic frontrunner. Clinton, a former First Lady, US Senator, and Secretary of State, brought extensive expertise to her campaign. She positioned herself as an advocate for progressive causes, concentrating on subjects such as healthcare reform, women's rights, and economic injustice. Clinton had substantial difficulties, including distrust from progressive voters who supported her primary opponent, Senator Bernie Sanders, as well as ongoing criticism over her use of a private email server as Secretary of State.

Donald Trump, a millionaire real estate magnate and reality TV celebrity, has launched his Republican candidacy. Many regarded Trump as a fringe contender, but he swiftly gained traction with a message that connected with disenfranchised people. He ran on a platform of economic nationalism, vowing to "Make America Great Again" by restoring manufacturing jobs, renegotiating trade agreements, and taking a harsh position on immigration. Trump's unvarnished manner, which included provocative remarks and a willingness to criticize both political opponents and the media, distinguished him from traditional politicians and invigorated a base of fans who felt ignored by the political elite.

The significance of the 2016 election in American history.

The 2016 election was noteworthy for a number of reasons. It showed fundamental differences in American culture, as well as the political system's vulnerability to disinformation and foreign influence. The election also demonstrated the rising power of social media and the shifting dynamics of political communication.

Hillary Clinton's candidacy was historic, since she became the first woman nominated for president by a major political party. Her campaign represented the continuous battle for gender equality in American politics.

Donald Trump's triumph, on the other hand, marked a significant shift in the political landscape. His victory was interpreted as a rejection of the political establishment and a challenge to the standards of presidential conduct and decorum. Trump's unusual campaign style, which emphasized social media and direct connection with supporters, transformed political campaigning and communication.

The election also has long-term ramifications for American democracy. The allegations of Russian meddling, which intended to influence the vote in Trump's favor, prompted questions about the election process's integrity and the role of foreign players in American politics. Furthermore, the controversial character of the election and its aftermath exacerbated political and social differences, laying the groundwork for future confrontations and debates.

In summary, the 2016 presidential election marked a watershed event in American history. It mirrored the complexities and problems of a rapidly evolving culture, reshaping the political landscape in ways that still impact American politics today. This book tries to offer a thorough analysis of this historic election, including its backdrop, important events, and long-term influence on the United States.

Chapter One:
The Early Contenders

Chapter One: The Early Contenders

Republican Primaries :

The Republican primaries of 2016 were a chaotic and tough election, with a crowded field of contenders and the unexpected ascension of a political outsider. This chapter will look at the important contenders, the responses to Donald Trump's entry into the race, the primary debates, and key moments that marked the early phases of the Republican election.

Key candidates include Jeb Bush, Ted Cruz, Marco Rubio, and Donald Trump.

Jeb Bush, the former governor of Florida and brother of President George W. Bush, began the contest as the frontrunner. Bush was viewed as a conservative, establishment candidate who could unite the party, thanks to his strong political background and huge fundraising powers. His agenda emphasized comprehensive immigration reform, education, and economic development. However, Bush failed to stand out in a crowded field and was chastised for his apparent lack of enthusiasm and charm.

Ted Cruz: Senator Ted Cruz of Texas was recognized for his fierce conservatism and willingness to take on the Republican establishment. Cruz appealed to the party's evangelical and Tea Party wings, emphasizing strict commitment to the Constitution, opposition to the Affordable Care Act, and a strong approach to immigration. His outsider status and reputation as a firebrand made him an extremely strong contender in the primaries.

Marco Rubio: Senator Marco Rubio of Florida presented himself as a new face for the Republican Party, giving a vision of a new generation of leaders. Rubio's compelling personal narrative as the son of Cuban immigrants struck a chord with many people. He prioritized programs encouraging economic opportunity, national security, and educational reform. Despite his initial popularity, Rubio struggled to retain momentum throughout the primaries.

Donald Trump's entry into the contest on June 16, 2015, sparked suspicion and interest. Many political observers first disregarded Trump, a businessman and reality TV personality with no prior political experience. However, his outspoken, unrepentant approach and populist message immediately won over a sizable segment of the Republican base. Trump vowed to "Make America Great Again" by reviving employment, renegotiating trade agreements, and taking a hard line on immigration and national security. His innovative campaign methods, which included regular use of social media, challenged established political norms and received widespread media attention.

Trump's Entry and Initial Reactions :

Trump's debut speech established the tone for his campaign, with big assertions and contentious comments, notably against immigration. He referred to Mexican immigrants as criminals and rapists, which sparked enormous outrage from many quarters but also resonated with people worried about immigration concerns. The political elite and media first dismissed Trump's campaign as a distraction, anticipating it to fail swiftly. However, his uncensored attitude and ability to dominate media coverage helped him gain a loyal following.

Trump's ascent in the polls surprised many of his opponents, forcing them to reevaluate their strategy. As Trump's support swelled, the Republican establishment and other contenders debated how to confront his unusual campaign.

Primary Debates and Key Moments

The Republican primary debates were influential in determining the election. They gave a venue for candidates to stand out and confront their opponents. Key moments include:

First debate (August 2015):

Fox News hosted the first debate, which featured 10 contenders. Trump instantly stood out, sparring with moderator Megyn Kelly over previous remarks about women. Despite the issue, his direct comments resounded among his admirers.

Jeb Bush's Struggle:

Bush's debate performances were largely seen as weak. He struggled to refute Trump's assaults and failed to create a convincing vision that would pique the party's interest.

Ted Cruz's Rise:

Cruz's excellent debate performances and ability to connect to Christian voters helped him win victory in areas like as Iowa. He positioned himself as a conservative alternative to Trump.

Marco Rubio's Fumble:

Rubio repeated a planned remark several times during a February debate, which Chris Christie emphasized, harming Rubio's reputation as an intelligent and spontaneous contender.

Democratic primaries :

The Democratic primaries were marked by a battle between a seasoned political heavyweight and an upstart campaign that invigorated the party's progressive wing. This section will look at Hillary Clinton's position as the leader, Bernie Sanders' surprising challenge, and the primary debates and major moments that shaped the campaign.

Hillary Clinton is the frontrunner.

Hillary Clinton was the presumptive Democratic nominee in the 2016 presidential election. Clinton's broad experience as a former First Lady, Senator, and Secretary of State earned her widespread respect and institutional backing. Her campaign centered on building on the Obama administration's accomplishments, with measures aiming at extending healthcare, increasing education, and combating wealth disparity. Clinton also highlighted her historic campaign as the probable first female president of the United States.

Despite her advantages, Clinton had tremendous hurdles. Her use of a private email server during her term as Secretary of State prompted an FBI investigation and continued scrutiny. Furthermore, her intimate links to Wall Street and the political elite made it difficult for her to connect with those who want more radical change.

Bernie Sanders' insurgent campaign

Senator Bernie Sanders of Vermont initiated a drive to rally the party's progressive side and challenge Clinton's supremacy. Sanders campaigned on a democratic socialist platform, advocating for programs such as universal healthcare, free public college tuition, and a $15 minimum wage. His message of tackling economic injustice and confronting the "billionaire class" resonated with many voters, particularly young people.

Sanders' grassroots campaign was mainly reliant on small-dollar donations, allowing him to compete financially against Clinton's well-funded organization. His genuineness and consistent message helped him acquire enormous traction, transforming what many saw as Clinton's coronation into a contested primary campaign.

Primary Debates and Key Moments

The Democratic primary debates gave an opportunity for Clinton and Sanders to express their agendas and contrast their tactics. Key moments include:

First debate (October 2015):

Sanders' statement that Americans were "sick and tired of hearing about [Clinton's] damn emails" helped change the conversation to substantive problems and garnered him plaudits for candor. Clinton demonstrated her policy understanding and experience.

Sanders' Momentum:

Sanders' surprising victory in the New Hampshire primary confirmed his status as a viable candidate. His ongoing performance in caucus states and among younger people reflected a dramatic change in the Democratic Party.

Clinton's resilience:

Despite Sanders' challenge, Clinton retained high support among minority voters, which was critical in her victory in important states. Her thorough policy ideas and emphasis on practical solutions helped to cement her position as the frontrunner.

Super Tuesday, March 2016:

Clinton's impressive showing on Super Tuesday, which included victories in numerous crucial states, secured her nomination bid. Sanders persisted, but the delegate math increasingly favored Clinton.

In conclusion, the early phases of the 2016 presidential campaign were defined by fierce rivalry and unexpected outcomes in both the Republican and Democratic primaries. The ascent of Donald Trump and Bernie Sanders mirrored widespread disillusionment with the political establishment, paving the way for a historic and controversial general election.

Chapter 2:
The Road to Nominations

Chapter 2: The Road to Nominations.

Republican Primary and Caucuses

The Republican primaries and caucuses of 2016 saw Donald Trump emerge as a dominating force, transforming the Republican Party and threatening its established power structure. This chapter will look at Trump's primary domination, important victories and setbacks, as well as the endorsements and withdrawals that defined the campaign.

Trump's dominance in the primaries

Donald Trump's unusual campaign style, highlighted by his use of social media, massive rallies, and inflammatory statements, rapidly distinguished him from his opponents. His platform of economic nationalism, anti-immigrant policies, and vows to "drain the swamp" appealed to a sizable percentage of the Republican Party, particularly white working-class people who felt estranged from the political elite.

Trump's supremacy became clear early in the primary season. His ability to attract media attention and his reluctance to follow traditional political rules enabled him to establish and maintain a significant lead in the polls. Despite multiple issues and assaults from his opponents, Trump has continued to exceed predictions and build his support.

Key Wins and Losses

Iowa caucuses (February 1, 2016):

Ted Cruz won the Iowa caucuses, defeating Donald Trump by a slim margin. This victory provided Cruz's campaign a tremendous boost and proved the strength of his evangelical voting base. However, Trump immediately recovered.

New Hampshire primary (February 9, 2016):

Trump easily won the New Hampshire primary, receiving 35.3% of the vote. This victory cemented his position as the frontrunner and provided him with valuable momentum moving into the upcoming games.

South Carolina primary (February 20, 2016):

Trump won the South Carolina primary with 32.5% of the vote, solidifying his lead. Marco Rubio and Ted Cruz came in a close second and third, respectively.

Super Tuesday (March 1, 2016)

Trump won seven of the eleven states that held primaries or caucuses on Super Tuesday, including Alabama, Arkansas, Georgia, Massachusetts, Tennessee, Vermont, and Virginia. His victories indicated widespread regional popularity and solidified his lead in the delegate count.

Florida's Primary (March 15, 2016):

Trump won the Florida primary with 45.7% of the vote, thereby terminating Marco Rubio's candidacy. This victory was especially noteworthy since it highlighted Trump's capacity to win in a crucial swing state.

Ohio primary (March 15, 2016):

John Kasich won Ohio, a rare defeat for Trump. Kasich's victory kept him in the race, but he failed to generate traction in other states.

Indiana primary (May 3, 2016):

Ted Cruz suspended his candidacy when Donald Trump won Indiana with 53.3% of the vote. This victory largely sealed Trump's route to the nomination.

Endorsements and Drop Outs

Jeb Bush:

Despite starting the race as the leader, Jeb Bush struggled to establish traction and withdrew following a poor result in the South Carolina primary. His resignation signaled the end of a major political dynasty's influence in the 2016 election.

Marco Rubio:

Rubio's campaign began with promise, but he struggled to retain momentum and eventually halted it after losing his home state of Florida to Trump.

Ted Cruz:

Cruz emerged as Trump's final real competitor, winning numerous states and gaining a sizable delegate total. However, his defeat in Indiana forced him to abandon his campaign, thus handing the candidacy to Trump.

John Kasich:

Kasich lasted the longest of Trump's opponents, winning just his own state of Ohio. He called off his campaign on May 4, 2016, after it became evident that he couldn't stop Trump from gaining the nomination.

As the primary season continued, Trump's ability to dominate media attention, appeal to alienated voters, and unusual strategy culminated to his election as Republican nominee, dramatically changing the party's future.

Democratic Primary and Caucuses

The 2016 Democratic primaries and caucuses saw a tough contest between Hillary Clinton and Bernie Sanders. This section will look at the contest's dynamics, including major victories and defeats, as well as endorsements and withdrawals that affected the race.

Clinton vs. Sanders: A Battle for the Soul of the Democratic Party

The primary campaign between Hillary Clinton and Bernie Sanders exposed profound ideological divides within the Democratic Party. Clinton, representing the party establishment, stressed her expertise and pragmatic approach. Sanders, on the other hand, pushed a progressive agenda centered on economic equality and institutional transformation.

Hillary Clinton's campaign centered on building on the Obama administration's successes, with comprehensive policy proposals on healthcare, education, and economic opportunity. She positioned herself as a stable and experienced leader capable of managing governance issues and implementing slow but substantive change.

Bernie Sanders: Sanders' campaign energized the party's progressive base with radical plans such as universal healthcare, free public college tuition, and a $15 minimum wage. His condemnation of wealth disparity and corporate money's dominance in politics struck a chord with many voters, particularly young people and those dissatisfied with the existing quo.

Key Wins and Losses

Iowa caucuses (February 1, 2016):

Clinton won the Iowa caucuses by a fraction of a point. The tight outcome underlined Sanders' rising popularity and paved the way for a tough primary season.

New Hampshire primary (February 9, 2016):

Sanders won the New Hampshire primary with 60.4% of the vote, proving his significant support among white, working-class, and young people. This victory significantly boosted his candidacy.

Super Tuesday (March 1, 2016)

Clinton won seven of the eleven states that had primaries or caucuses on Super Tuesday, including Alabama, Arkansas, Georgia, Massachusetts, Tennessee, Texas, and Virginia. Her victories in Southern states were especially remarkable, demonstrating her widespread popularity among African American voters.

Michigan's Primary (March 8, 2016):

Sanders scored a major shock by winning the Michigan primary, defying polling predictions and demonstrating that his message resonated in the industrial Midwest. This victory energized his campaign and highlighted his popularity among working-class voters.

New York primary (April 19, 2016):

Clinton won the New York primary with 57.5% of the vote, a significant victory in her home state that cemented her delegate advantage. The victory highlighted her popularity in varied urban regions.

California primary (June 7, 2016):

Clinton won the California primary with 53.1% of the vote, essentially ending Sanders' bid for the candidacy. Her triumph in the nation's most populous state demonstrated her vast base of support.

Endorsements and Drop Outs

Martin O'Malley:

Former Maryland Governor Martin O'Malley entered the campaign as a long shot contender. His candidacy struggled to get traction, and he suspended it following a bad performance in the Iowa caucuses.

Key Endorsements for Clinton:

Clinton garnered support from notable Democratic personalities such as President Barack Obama, Vice President Joe Biden, and previous presidential candidates John Kerry and Al Gore. These endorsements boosted her campaign's legitimacy and showed party unity.

Key Sanders Endorsements:

Sanders has attracted support from leftist groups and individuals, including the Democratic Socialists of America, National Nurses United, and notable intellectuals such as Cornel West and Noam Chomsky. These endorsements invigorated his grassroots supporters.

Despite Sanders' strong challenge and the excitement of his followers, Clinton won the Democratic nomination because to her delegate advantage and large coalition. The race emphasized the rising dominance of progressive views inside the Democratic Party, laying the groundwork for a heated general election against Trump.

To summarize, the 2016 presidential nomination process was distinguished by unexpected developments and strong rivalry in both the Republican and Democratic primaries. Donald Trump's dominance and unconventional approach changed the Republican Party, while Hillary Clinton's ideological struggle with Bernie Sanders exposed major splits within the Democratic Party. These factors pave the way for a historic and controversial general election campaign.

Chapter Three: The Conventions

Chapter Three: The Conventions

Republican National Convention

The 2016 Republican National Convention (RNC) was held in Cleveland, Ohio, from July 18 to 21. This chapter will go over major speeches and situations, the status of party unity and differences, and the nominations of Donald Trump and Mike Pence.

Key speeches and moments.

The RNC included a mix of conventional speeches from party elders, emerging stars, and Trump family members. Some of the most notable moments were:

Melania Trump's Speech:

Melania Trump gave a well-received address on the first night, although it was later uncovered that portions of it were copied from Michelle Obama's 2008 Democratic National Convention speech. The issue overshadowed the excellent portions of her speech.

Rudy Giuliani:

Former New York City Mayor Rudy Giuliani delivered a passionate address in support of Trump, emphasizing law and order and portraying him as a strong leader capable of restoring America's safety.

Chris Christie:

New Jersey Governor Chris Christie staged a fake "prosecution" of Hillary Clinton, inciting the audience in cries of "Lock her up!" This event summed up the convention's anger for Clinton.

Ted Cruz's non-endorsement

Senator Ted Cruz, Trump's former primary opponent, delivered a speech in which he specifically did not endorse Trump, instead urged Republicans to "vote your conscience." Cruz was booed off the stage, underlining the party's remaining differences.

Donald Trump's acceptance speech:

On the last night of the convention, Trump delivered the longest acceptance speech in modern history. He portrayed a bleak picture of America, highlighting crime, terrorism, and economic collapse, and positioned himself as the man capable of restoring peace and prosperity. His rhetoric appealed to his following, but opponents saw it as unduly harsh and fear-mongering.

Party Unity and Divisions

The RNC revealed both the Republican Party's unity and divides. While the convention effectively demonstrated Trump's backing from many prominent Republicans, it also revealed substantial rifts:

Unity:

Key officials like as House Speaker Paul Ryan and Senate Majority Leader Mitch McConnell backed Trump's candidacy, hoping to show a united front against Hillary Clinton.

Trump's ability to draw big audiences and ardent followers revealed a solid grassroots foundation inside the party.

Divisions:

The convention showed profound splits, notably Ted Cruz's unwillingness to embrace Trump and the audience's divided reactions.

Several notable Republicans, including former Presidents George H.W. Bush and George W. Bush, as well as 2012 nominee Mitt Romney, were noticeably missing, expressing their opposition to Trump.

Nomination of Donald Trump and Mike Pence

The RNC culminated with Donald Trump's formal selection as the Republican presidential nominee, with Indiana Governor Mike Pence serving as his running mate. Pence, a socially conservative and experienced politician, was picked to help balance the ticket and appeal to traditional Republicans. The nominating procedure involved:

Roll Call Vote:

The roll call vote on July 19 validated Trump's candidacy. Trump earned 1,725 delegates, much over the 1,237 required to win the nomination.

Vice Presidential Nominations:

On July 20, Mike Pence accepted the nomination for vice president, delivering a speech emphasizing his conservative credentials and support to Trump.

The RNC finished with a fireworks show and a feeling of excitement about the general election campaign.

Democrat National Convention

The 2016 Democratic National Convention (DNC) took place in Philadelphia, Pennsylvania, on July 25-28. This section will go over major speeches and incidents, the status of party unity and splits, and the nominations of Hillary Clinton and Tim Kaine.

Key speeches and moments.

The DNC included a number of impressive and poignant speeches from notable Democrats, celebrities, and Clinton family members. Key moments include:

Michelle Obama's Speech:

The First Lady gave a critically lauded speech emphasizing the value of strong role models and inclusion. Her statement, "When they go low, we go high," became a rallying cry for Democrats.

Bernie Sanders Speech:

Sanders, Clinton's primary adversary, gave a speech in which he urged his supporters to rally behind Clinton in order to defeat Trump. His endorsement was critical to party unity, albeit some of his fans were suspicious.

Elizabeth Warren:

Senator Elizabeth Warren criticized Trump's corporate practices and supported Clinton's progressive platform. Her address was intended to energize the party's left side.

Bill Clinton's speech:

Former President Bill Clinton gave a personal and sympathetic portrayal of his wife's work and personality, describing her as a dedicated advocate for children and families.

Barack Obama's Speech:

President Barack Obama gave Clinton a passionate support, emphasizing her qualities and experience while contrasting them with those of Trump. Obama's address was interpreted as a handing of the mantle to Clinton.

Hillary Clinton's Acceptance speech:

On the last night, Clinton accepted the candidacy, becoming the first woman nominated for president by a major political party. Her address focused on her vision for America, emphasizing unity, inclusion, and building on the achievements of the Obama administration.

Party Unity and Divisions

The DNC emphasized attempts to unite the party following a rocky primary season, but it also revealed some persistent divisions:

Unity:

The participation and support of significant leaders such as Bernie Sanders, Elizabeth Warren, and Barack Obama contributed create a cohesive front. Their endorsements were critical to bringing the party together.

The historic aspect of Clinton's candidacy inspired many Democrats, particularly women and young people.

Divisions:

Some Sanders supporters were outspoken in their opposition to Clinton, holding rallies inside and outside the conference. The publication of DNC emails indicating bias against Sanders heightened their outrage.

Efforts were made to bridge these gaps by putting progressive ideals into the party platform and emphasizing points of agreement.

Nominations for Hillary Clinton and Tim Kaine

The DNC's highlight was Hillary Clinton's formal selection as the Democratic presidential nominee, with Virginia Senator Tim Kaine serving as her running mate. Kaine, a moderate Democrat with foreign policy expertise and a track record of collaboration, was picked to appeal to a diverse range of voters. The nominating procedure involved:

Roll Call Vote:

On July 26, a roll-call vote affirmed Clinton's selection. Clinton garnered 2,842 delegates and won the nomination by a wide majority.

Vice Presidential Nominations:

On July 27, Tim Kaine accepted the vice presidential nomination, making a speech emphasizing his public service history and his shared beliefs with Hillary Clinton.

The DNC closed with a joyful environment characterized by confetti, balloons, and a sense of optimism as the party prepared for the general election.

To summarize, the conventions were pivotal milestones in the 2016 election, highlighting the candidates and their ambitions for America. The RNC highlighted the Republican Party's divides but eventually united around Trump, whereas the DNC emphasized unity and inclusion, celebrating Clinton's historic nomination. Both conventions laid the groundwork for a hotly contested general election campaign.

Chapter 4: General Election Campaign

Chapter 4: General Election Campaign

Campaign Strategy

Clinton's Strategy: Experience, Policy, and Inclusion

Hillary Clinton's campaign approach focused on her broad political experience, specific policy ideas, and message of inclusion. The major components of her plan included:

Experience:

Clinton emphasized her decades-long career in public service, which included positions as First Lady, Senator, and Secretary of State. She presented herself as a stable and capable leader with the expertise required to overcome complicated foreign and domestic difficulties.

Policy proposals:

Clinton's campaign had extensive policy recommendations on a variety of areas, including healthcare, education, climate change, and economic injustice. Her initiatives sought to build on the accomplishments of the Obama administration while also addressing the concerns of working families.

Inclusivity:

Clinton's inclusive platform sought to unite multiple voter coalitions, including women, minorities, LGBTQ+ folks, and young people. Her campaign motto, "Stronger Together," captured her vision of a unified and inclusive America.

Ground Game:

The Clinton team made significant investments in the ground game, with an emphasis on voter registration, outreach, and mobilization. This includes large funding for battleground states and critical demographic groupings.

Trump's Strategy: Outsider Status, Populism, and Media Domination.

Donald Trump's campaign approach emphasized his outsider status, populist rhetoric, and ability to dominate media attention. The major components of his plan were:

Outsider Status:

Trump portrayed himself as a political outsider who would upend the established order and "drain the swamp" of Washington corruption. His lack of political experience was positioned as an advantage, appealing to those dissatisfied with established politics.

Populist rhetoric:

Trump's campaign centered on economic nationalism, anti-immigrant policies, and a heavy emphasis on law and order. His rhetoric appealed to working-class people who felt left behind by globalization and technological advancement.

Media Domination:

Trump's ability to capture media attention with controversial speeches and rallies enabled him to control the news cycle. His use of social media, namely Twitter, allowed him to engage directly with voters while avoiding traditional media censors.

Simple messaging:

Trump's campaign employed simple, memorable slogans like "Make America Great Again" and "Build the Wall" to express his major points. This technique helped him build a strong, consistent brand that resonated with his target audience.

Media Coverage

Traditional media versus social media.

The 2016 election marked a dramatic shift in how campaigns and candidates interacted with the media, with conventional media sources and social media platforms playing important roles.

Traditional Media:

Traditional media outlets, including television networks, newspapers, and radio, provided significant coverage of the election. However, the tone of this coverage varied greatly, with some publications offering critical appraisals of the candidates and others being accused of prejudice or sensationalism.

Social Media:

Facebook, Twitter, and Instagram all played important roles in the election. Both campaigns utilized these media to reach voters, but Trump's team excelled at utilizing Twitter to set the agenda and respond to major developments in real time.

Influence of Social Media:

Social media enabled the speedy broadcast of information and provided a platform for direct voter participation. However, technology also aided in the dissemination of disinformation and polarized the electorate.

The role of "fake news" and misinformation.

"Fake News" :

The phrase "fake news" gained popularity during the 2016 election, referring to the dissemination of incorrect or misleading information, generally with the purpose to deceive. This situation was exacerbated by social media algorithms that encouraged sensationalized material.

The impact of misinformation:

Misinformation efforts, particularly those related to foreign entities, aimed to sway voter attitudes and promote division. False tales about both candidates spread rapidly, confounding efforts to separate reality from fiction.

Response to misinformation:

To counteract disinformation, media organizations launched fact-checking campaigns and intensified scrutiny of social media platforms' involvement in distributing incorrect information. However, these efforts encountered substantial hurdles.

Key Campaign Events:

Rallies, Debate, and Controversy

Rallies:

Both candidates staged several rallies around the country, utilizing them to inspire their supporters and convey their views. Trump rallies were renowned for his enormous audiences and ardent followers, whilst Clinton rallies focused on policy and inclusion.

Debates:

The three presidential debates were pivotal events in the campaign. These debates addressed a variety of themes, including the economy, healthcare, foreign policy, and character concerns. Clinton was widely seen as the better prepared and collected candidate, but Trump utilized the debates to underscore his outsider status and confront Clinton directly.

Controversies:

Both efforts generated major controversy. Clinton's campaign was plagued by the ongoing email controversy, whereas Trump faced several claims of wrongdoing, including the revelation of the Access Hollywood tape.

The Email Scandal and the "Lock Her Up" Chant

Email Scandal:

The controversy over Clinton's use of a private email server as Secretary of State dominated the campaign. The FBI launched an investigation and determined that, while Clinton was "extremely careless," no criminal charges were merited.

Impact on Campaign:

The email issue hampered Clinton's campaign, adding to impressions of untrustworthiness. Trump's campaign seized on this topic, constantly calling for Clinton's imprisonment.

"Lock Her Up" Chants

The term "Lock her up" became a popular chant at Trump rallies, expressing his followers' strong antipathy for Clinton. This rhetoric was a key component of Trump's effort to delegitimize Clinton and motivate his supporters.

The Access Hollywood tape and Its Impact

Release of the tape:

On October 7, 2016, The Washington Post published a 2005 tape of Trump making vulgar remarks about women, including bragging about touching them without their consent. The publication of the Access Hollywood footage sparked a massive outcry.

Public and Political Reactions:

The recording was widely condemned by both Democrats and Republicans. Many prominent Republicans, including those who had embraced Trump, publicly denounced him, with some calling for his withdrawal from the race.

Impact on the Campaign:

Despite the early response, Trump weathered the storm. He offered a public apology and attempted to divert attention by criticizing Clinton and emphasizing topics vital to his supporters. The episode revealed his supporters' tenacity as well as the electorate's polarization.

To summarize, the 2016 general election campaign was defined by divergent strategy, extensive media coverage, and critical events that affected the race. Clinton's emphasis on expertise and policy contrasted with Trump's outsider appeal and media savvy approach. The role of social media and the propagation of disinformation complicated the campaign, while issues such as the email scandal and the Access Hollywood tape had a significant impact on voter impressions and, eventually, election outcomes.

Chapter 5:
The Debates.

Chapter 5: The Debates.

The 2016 presidential debates were watershed moments in the campaign, offering voters direct comparisons of the candidates' views, temperament, and ability to manage pressure. This chapter explores the major events and assessments of each debate, including the vice presidential debate.

First Presidential Debate.

The first presidential debate was held on September 26, 2016, at Hofstra University in Hempstead, New York. It was one of the most viewed debates in US history, with an estimated 84 million people. It was moderated by NBC's Lester Holt.

Key Moments

Opening statements:

Hillary Clinton presented herself as an experienced public servant with a detailed strategy to boost the economy, help small companies, and assure equal pay for women. She focused on her experience and comprehensive policy ideas.

Donald Trump positioned himself as a successful businessman who could bring new ideas to Washington. He emphasized trade deals, job creation, and his intention to renegotiate or withdraw from international accords such as NAFTA.

Economy and trade:

Clinton discussed her proposals for job creation through investments in sustainable energy, infrastructure, and technology. She slammed Trump's tax proposals as benefiting the rich.

Trump criticized Clinton's support for trade agreements, blaming them for job losses and economic downturns in industrialized areas. He touted his potential to renegotiate better terms for America.

Race Relations and Police:

Clinton advocated for criminal justice reform, community policing, and confronting systematic racism. She advocated for increased trust between law enforcement and communities.

Trump stressed law and order, promoting stop-and-frisk measures and defending the police. He created a picture of escalating criminality that required drastic measures to fight.

Temperament and preparation:

Clinton questioned Trump's temperament and readiness to be president, citing his provocative words and actions. She argued that he was unsuited for office.

Trump criticized Clinton's past, particularly her use of a private email server, and questioned her judgment. He felt she lacked the stamina to become president.

Analysis

Clinton's Performance:

Clinton was usually seen as the better-prepared and calm candidate. Her debating expertise and in-depth policy understanding showed through. She expertly answered Trump's attacks while remaining cool.

Trump's Performance:

Trump was chastised for his interruptions and lack of specific policy understanding. However, his plain-spoken demeanor and outsider status remained appealing to his followers. Some believed he successfully depicted Clinton as part of the establishment issue.

Second Presidential Debate.

The second presidential debate was held on October 9, 2016, at Washington University in St. Louis, Missouri. Martha Raddatz of ABC News and Anderson Cooper of CNN moderated the town hall, which included questions from both moderators and undecided voters in the audience.

Key Moments

Opening Tensions:

The discussion came only days after the revelation of the Access Hollywood tape, in which Trump was heard making vulgar remarks about women. This generated a very charged environment from the start.

Trump opened the discussion in an unorthodox way, holding a news conference with women who accused Bill Clinton of sexual misconduct in a bid to divert attention away from his own issue.

Health Care:

Clinton defended the Affordable Care Act (ACA) and suggested changes, such as cost reductions and increased coverage. She attacked Trump's intention to dismantle the ACA without providing a suitable successor.

Trump restated his commitment to repeal and replace the ACA, calling it a failure. He made vague statements about cutting expenses and promoting competition, but lacked specifics.

Immigration:

Trump reiterated his ambitions to build a wall along the US-Mexico border and impose harsher immigration regulations. He characterized the issue as one of national security and economic preservation.

Clinton supported comprehensive immigration reform, including a route to citizenship for unauthorized immigrants. She stressed immigrants' contributions to American culture.

Foreign policy:

Clinton discussed her expertise and proposals for dealing with Russia, ISIS, and other global issues. She accused Trump of being unprepared to tackle complicated foreign challenges.

Trump slammed Clinton's record, notably her time as Secretary of State, and accused her of aiding to the growth of ISIS. He advocated for bolder military action and better relationships.

Analysis

Clinton's Performance:

Despite the debate's hostile tone, Clinton remained controlled and attentive. She proceeded to stress her experience and in-depth policy understanding.

Trump's Performance:

Trump took a more aggressive approach, aggressively criticizing Clinton on several fronts. While his style was perceived as aggressive, it emphasized his outsider status and readiness to challenge the system.

Third Presidential Debate.

The third and final presidential debate was held on October 19, 2016, at the University of Nevada in Las Vegas. Chris Wallace of Fox News moderated the discussion, which was largely focused on policy topics.

Key Moments

Supreme Court:

Clinton underlined the need of picking judges who will protect Roe v. Wade and advance progressive ideas. She portrayed the Supreme Court as critical to defending rights and liberties.

Trump prioritized picking conservative justices who would overturn Roe v. Wade and uphold the Second Amendment. He advocated the rigorous interpretation of the Constitution.

Economy:

Clinton restated her proposals to lower taxes for the middle class, invest in infrastructure, and raise the minimum wage. She attacked Trump's tax proposal, claiming that it benefits the rich.

Trump pledged significant tax cuts, deregulation, and renegotiated trade agreements. He depicted Clinton as a member of the establishment whose policies had failed to generate economic development.

Election Integrity:

Clinton defended the integrity of the electoral process and accused Trump of harming democracy by implying that the election might be rigged.

Trump made headlines for refusing to accept the election results, declaring, "I will keep you in suspense." This unprecedented position sparked fears about a peaceful transition of power.

Foreign Policy and National Security:

Clinton stressed her experience and outlined her strategies for combating global concerns like as cybersecurity and terrorism.

Trump slammed Clinton's record, namely the Iran nuclear agreement and the emergence of ISIS. He vowed to take more decisive action on national security.

Analysis

Clinton's Performance:

Clinton was seen as calm, educated, and presidential. She skillfully communicated her policy opinions while maintaining a calm tone.

Trump's Performance:

Donald Trump's unwillingness to recognize the election results received widespread attention and condemnation. His hardline attitude resonated to his supporters while alienating some undecided voters.

Vice President's Debate

The vice presidential debate was held on October 4, 2016, at Longwood University in Farmville, Virginia. Elaine Quijano of CBS News moderated the discussion, which included Senator Tim Kaine and Governor Mike Pence.

Key Moments

Opening statements:

Tim Kaine underlined Clinton's and his own leadership experience and preparation. He criticized Trump and Pence's policies and actions.

Mike Pence focused on his and Trump's promises to boost the economy, restore law and order, and bring about change in Washington. He painted Clinton and Kaine as members of the failing establishment.

Economy and Taxation:

Kaine praised Clinton's economic ideas, emphasizing middle-class tax cuts as well as infrastructure and clean energy investments. He slammed Trump's tax proposal as favoring the wealthy.

Pence touted Trump's tax cuts, deregulation, and commitment to renegotiate trade agreements. He presented their economic strategy as a method to stimulate growth and generate jobs.

National security and foreign policy:

Kaine underlined Clinton's experience and outlined her proposals for dealing with global issues. He chastised Trump for his lack of experience and provocative views on foreign affairs.

Pence praised Trump's foreign policy ideas, emphasizing a robust military and decisive action against ISIS. He criticized Clinton's record, namely her handling of the Benghazi incident.

Character and temperament:

Kaine constantly questioned Trump's temperament and aptitude for the president, citing Trump's own statements against him.

Pence stayed cool and collected, dismissing assaults on Trump's character and instead emphasizing substantive differences. His manner was in stark contrast to Trump's more aggressive style.

Analysis

Kaine's Performance:

Kaine's forceful attitude and repeated interruptions were seen less successful. While he succeeded in raising questions about Trump's character, his technique was critiqued for being unpolished.

Pence's Performance:

Pence was largely seen as the winner of the debate. His calm, steady manner and solid support of Trump assuaged many Republican voters. He successfully conveyed a feeling of steadiness and expertise.

In conclusion, the debates were critical in molding voter impressions and emphasizing the substantial differences between the contenders. Clinton's focus on expertise and policy contrasted with Trump's outsider appeal and populist rhetoric. The vice presidential debate showcased the running mates' ability to defend their respective tickets and connect with voters. These debates shaped the closing weeks of the campaign and affected the election's outcome.

Chapter 6: Controversies and Scandals.

Chapter 6: Controversies and Scandals.

Numerous controversies and scandals dominated the 2016 presidential campaign, having a substantial influence on both candidates and overall election dynamics. This chapter dives into the key political controversies involving Hillary Clinton and Donald Trump, as well as the larger topic of Russian electoral intervention.

Hillary Clinton's Email Scandal

Background

Private Email Servers:

The scandal arose when it was revealed that Hillary Clinton utilized a private email server for official correspondence while serving as Secretary of State from 2009 to 2013. This sparked worries regarding the protection of sensitive data and adherence to federal records rules.

FBI investigation:

In 2015, the FBI initiated an investigation into Clinton's email habits to see if any sensitive material was mishandled. In July 2016, FBI Director James Comey declared that the investigation was complete and that no charges would be filed, while he condemned Clinton's handling of sensitive material as "extremely careless".

Impact on the Campaign

Trustworthiness:

The email issue severely harmed Clinton's credibility and fed claims of her untrustworthiness and lack of openness. Polls continually revealed that many people thought she was dishonest.

Media Coverage:

The incident received widespread media attention throughout the campaign, putting it in the public spotlight. This continual scrutiny hampered Clinton's efforts to concentrate on policy concerns and her vision for the country.

Reopening the investigation:

Just days before the election, on October 28, 2016, Comey revealed that the FBI was reviving the case after discovering new emails. Although he subsequently stated that the review did not modify the FBI's initial finding, the timing of the revelation heightened the uncertainty and controversy surrounding Clinton.

Voter Impact:

The increased attention on the email controversy in the final days of the campaign is said to have affected undecided voters and led to a drop in excitement among Clinton supporters. The dispute may have contributed to the thin margins in critical swing states that finally swung the election.

Donald Trump's Personal Conduct

The Access Hollywood tape

Release of the tape:

On October 7, 2016, The Washington Post published a 2005 audio in which Trump made obscene and sexually aggressive remarks about women, including bragging about touching them without their consent. The recording, made during a chat with TV personality Billy Bush, drew immediate uproar.

Public and Political Reactions:

The recording was widely condemned by both Democrats and Republicans. Many notable Republicans, including those who had embraced Trump, distanced themselves from his remarks, while others urged for his withdrawal from the campaign.

Allegations of misconduct

Multiple accusations:

Throughout the campaign, many women accused Trump of sexual misbehavior, including unwelcome approaches, groping, and assault. Trump disputed all claims and promised to sue his accusers.

Impact on Campaign:

Despite the seriousness of the claims, Trump's core followers remained mostly faithful. His campaign sought to distract attention by questioning the authenticity of the women and emphasizing Bill Clinton's previous wrongdoing.

Media and Public Perception:

The Access Hollywood tape and following claims received widespread coverage in the media, further polarizing public opinion. For many voters, these incidents highlighted worries about Trump's character and suitability for office, but his supporters regarded them as part of a larger campaign to discredit his candidacy.

Russian Interference.

Overview of Russian Activities.

Hacking and Information Warfare:

Throughout the campaign, there were claims of Russian cyber actions intended to influence the election. These efforts included hacking the Democratic National Committee (DNC) and Clinton campaign chairman John Podesta's emails, which were later published by Wikileaks.

Disinformation campaigns:

Russian operatives utilized social media sites to disseminate misinformation, establish phony accounts, and amplify divisive messages. These activities were intended to foment dissension among American voters and weaken trust in the democratic process.

Impact on Public Perception and Campaign Dynamics.

Clinton Campaign:

The publication of leaked emails dealt a serious blow to the Clinton campaign. The emails' revelations prompted DNC Chair Debbie Wasserman Schultz's resignation and served as grist for Trump's assaults on Clinton's honesty and openness.

Trump's Campaign:

Trump and his team frequently minimized the severity of Russian meddling, with Trump memorably asking Russia to locate Clinton's "missing" emails during a news conference. This approach sparked concerns about his willingness to recognize and confront foreign meddling in the election.

Intelligence Community Assessment:

In January 2017, the US intelligence community issued a report indicating that Russia intervened in the 2016 election to undermine Clinton and aid Trump. This evaluation exacerbated arguments over the election's validity and the scope of foreign interference.

Public Reaction:

The topic of Russian influence became a major source of dispute, with sentiments sharply divided along political lines. Many Democrats perceived the intervention as a major threat to democracy, while many Republicans dismissed it as an exaggerated or politically driven concern.

Legislative and investigative Responses:

Numerous investigations into Russian influence were launched, notably by Congress and Special Counsel Robert Mueller. These investigations aimed to determine the scope of Russian actions and any possible coordination between the Trump campaign and Russian operatives.

In conclusion, the 2016 presidential campaign was heavily influenced by controversies and scandals involving both main contenders. Clinton's email controversy and Trump's personal behavior were critical topics that affected voter impressions and influenced election results. Furthermore, Russian meddling added a complicated and unusual dimension to the campaign, raising worries about the integrity of the election process and foreign actors' effect on American democracy.

Chapter 7:
The Final Stretch.

Chapter 7: The Final Stretch.

The final several weeks before Election Day were fraught with tremendous activity, unanticipated occurrences, and swings in voter attitude. This chapter delves into the important events and dynamics of the 2016 presidential campaign's final stretch, with an emphasis on "October Surprises," last-minute campaign activities, and an examination of polling data and forecasts.

October surprises

FBI Director James Comey's Announcements

Reopening the Email Investigation:

On October 28, 2016, FBI Director James Comey informed Congress that the FBI had uncovered fresh emails from Hillary Clinton's private email server. These emails were discovered on the laptop of former Congressman Anthony Weiner, Clinton aide Huma Abedin's estranged husband.

The news sparked a media tempest and rekindled debate about Clinton's email usage. The timing of the disclosure, barely 11 days before the election, was extremely detrimental, prompting debate about the influence on undecided voters.

Conclusion of the Investigation:

On November 6, 2016, just two days before the election, Comey wrote another letter to Congress, noting that the FBI's assessment of the newly found emails was complete and did not modify the agency's initial decision not to prosecute Clinton.

While this notification attempted to clarify the issue, it accomplished little to offset the harm caused by the original revelation. The resumption of the probe had already dominated the news and affected voter opinions.

Last Minute Campaign Efforts

Clinton Campaign:

In reaction to the growing email scandal, the Clinton team stepped up its attempts to focus on policy matters and rally supporters. Clinton and her surrogates campaigned hard in crucial swing states, highlighting her experience and contrasting it with Trump's.

High-profile supporters, including President Barack Obama and First Lady Michelle Obama, were instrumental in mobilizing Democratic voters and appealing to important groups like as African Americans, Latinos, and young people.

Trump's Campaign:

The Trump team took advantage of the rekindled email scandal, using it to reinforce their narrative of Clinton as dishonest and untrustworthy. Trump repeatedly brought up the inquiry in his speeches, casting it as proof of a crooked system.

Trump's campaign centered on motivating his base and gaining support among undecided voters in swing areas. He organized enormous rallies around the country, highlighting his outsider status and promising to "drain the swamp" in Washington.

Polls and Predictions

Analysis of Polling Data

National polls:

Throughout the campaign, national polls consistently showed Hillary Clinton leading Donald Trump by various amounts. However, the advantage shifted, particularly in the last weeks, due to the email incident and other events.

While Clinton maintained a stable advantage in the popular vote, the percentages tightened as Election Day neared, indicating a tight fight.

Swing State Polls:

Polls in crucial battleground states like as Florida, Pennsylvania, Michigan, Wisconsin, and Ohio had a vital role in determining the election results. These states demonstrated a more competitive election, with Trump gaining momentum in some key regions.

Polling data showed that Trump's message resonated with white working-class voters, particularly in Rust Belt areas. Clinton's campaign concentrated on urban areas and minority votes, but it had difficulties in rural and suburban areas.

Predictions and expectations.

Political analysts and pundits:

Most political experts and commentators projected Clinton's win, citing her national poll lead and demographic edge in crucial states. Many others assumed that Trump's route to success was limited and relied on switching historically Democratic states.

Experts agreed that Clinton's massive campaign infrastructure and seasoned team would ensure her presidency, but Trump's unorthodox approach was viewed as a big danger.

E

lection models and forecasts:

Several election models and projections, including those from FiveThirtyEight, The New York Times, and other media sites, predicted a high possibility of Clinton winning. These models calculated probability by combining polling data, historical patterns, and other variables.

While several models predicted a tighter race, Clinton remained the frontrunner in the majority of forecasts. The electoral map appeared to favor Hillary, with many pathways to the necessary 270 electoral votes.

Market and Public Sentiment:

Financial markets and betting odds also pointed to a Clinton triumph, reflecting broader popular mood and trust in her candidacy's durability.

However, there was a sense of uncertainty and instability, with many voters dissatisfied with both candidates. This unstable environment added to the challenge of generating precise forecasts.

In conclusion, the last stretch of the 2016 presidential campaign was marked by spectacular changes and fervent efforts by both candidates. The October Surprises, particularly Comey's statements, had a tremendous impact on defining the narrative and voter perception. Despite polling data and expert projections that Clinton would win, the election's outcome remained unknown, underscoring the race's unpredictable character and the wide differences within the American population.

Chapter 8,
Election Day

Chapter 8, Election Day

Election Day 2016 marked the end of a lengthy and controversial campaign packed with excitement, fear, and intensive activity across the United States. This chapter discusses the voting process, major battleground states, voter participation and demographics, and the sequence of events on Election Night, as well as responses from politicians and the general public.

The Voting Process

Key battleground states.

Importance of Swing States:

The 2016 election rested on a few crucial battleground states, sometimes known as swing states, where the outcome remained unclear, and both candidates concentrated their last campaign efforts. These states were Florida, Pennsylvania, Michigan, Wisconsin, North Carolina, and Ohio.

Florida:

Florida, a perennial swing state with a vast and varied population, was a significant prize, receiving 29 electoral votes. Both candidates campaigned extensively here, with immigration, healthcare, and the economy taking center stage.

PA, MI, and WI:

These usually Democratic states in the Rust Belt were critical battlegrounds. Many people in these states responded positively to Trump's rhetoric of economic nationalism and pledges to restart manufacturing.

North Carolina:

North Carolina, with its fast rising population and shifting demographics, was yet another important battleground. Jobs, education, and social policy were vigorously disputed.

Ohio:

Ohio, seen as a bellwether state, had a strong demand for its 18 electoral votes. Trump's appeal to working-class voters, as well as his emphasis on trade and industry, were key factors in this outcome.

Voter turnout and demographics

Overall turnout:

Approximately 138 million Americans voted in the 2016 election, accounting for around 58% of the eligible voting population. Voter turnout varied widely among states and demographic groups.

Demographic Breakdown:

Race and ethnicity:

African American attendance fell somewhat compared to 2012, but Latino and Asian American turnout rose. White voters, particularly those without a college degree, turned out in big numbers and were an important constituency for Trump.

Gender:

Women, particularly college-educated women, overwhelmingly backed Clinton, but males, particularly white men without a college degree, favored Trump.

Age:

Younger voters tended to back Clinton, although turnout was lower than expected. Older people were more inclined to vote for Trump.

Voter suppression and access:

Voter suppression and access were major concerns, with allegations of lengthy lineups, defective voting machines, and draconian voter ID legislation in several jurisdictions. These concerns disproportionately impacted minorities and low-income voters.

Election Night

Timeline of Events

Early evening:

Polls on the East Coast began closing at 7 p.m. EST, and the first results arrived shortly after. Initial results indicated a contested campaign, with both candidates winning projected states.

Swing State Results:

As results from critical battleground states began to arrive, the race tightened. Trump won Florida, North Carolina, and Ohio, putting him on track to receive 270 electoral votes.

Midnight and beyond:

The attention switched to Rust Belt states. Pennsylvania, Michigan, and Wisconsin, which had previously leaned Democratic, shown surprise support for Trump. As the night went on, it became evident that Trump was surpassing forecasts in these key states.

Reactions of Candidates and the Public

Clinton Campaign:

The Clinton team was initially certain of victory, but the surprise results in crucial states caught them off guard. As the night progressed and Trump's advantage cemented, the tone changed to one of shock and sadness. Clinton elected not to address her supporters that evening, instead waiting until the next morning to concede.

Trump's Campaign:

The attitude at Trump Tower was first hesitant, but became more celebratory as the results poured in. By early morning, it was evident that Trump had received enough electoral votes to win the president. Trump delivered his victory address, vowing to be the president of all Americans and to restore the country.

Public Reaction:

The public's reaction was quite split. Trump supporters celebrated what they perceived as a historic and revolutionary triumph, while Clinton backers and many others were stunned and disappointed with the outcome. Protests and protests occurred in various locations, highlighting the country's fundamental differences.

Media and analysts:

Political analysts and the media tried to make sense of the surprising outcome. The outcome contradicted most pre-election surveys and projections, sparking significant analysis and discussion regarding the variables that contributed to Trump's win, such as the importance of the electoral college, voter demographics, and the impact of controversies and outside involvement.

In conclusion, Election Day 2016 was a spectacular and momentous event that reflected the campaign's heated and frequently divided tone. The election process highlighted crucial battleground states and substantial demographic shifts, while Election Night was a rollercoaster of emotions and surprising results. The reactions of the candidates, the public, and the media highlighted the election's significant influence on the American political scene.

Chapter 9:
The
Aftermath

Chapter 9: The Aftermath

The aftermath of the 2016 presidential election was characterized by intense scrutiny, responses, and the start of a power shift from President Barack Obama to President-elect Donald Trump. This chapter examines the election results, reactions, and protests both locally and abroad, as well as the early stages of power transfer.

Election Results.

Electoral College versus Popular Vote

Electoral College Outcome:

Donald Trump won the presidency with 304 electoral votes to Hillary Clinton's 227. Trump achieved his triumph by capturing important battleground states including Florida, Pennsylvania, Michigan, and Wisconsin, which had previously voted Democratic.

Popular Vote Discrepancy

Despite losing the electoral college, Hillary Clinton won the popular vote by roughly 2.9 million votes, with 48.2% of all votes cast to Trump's 46.1%. This difference rekindled discussions about the electoral college system and its influence on democracy.

A breakdown of key states

Florida:

Trump's success in Florida, a key swing state with 29 electoral votes, was critical to his broader electoral college plan. His popularity to Hispanic and older voters, along with Clinton's underperformance in key demographics, helped him secure a close victory.

PA, MI, and WI:

Many analysts were surprised by Trump's gains in these normally Democratic-leaning states, which helped him win. His message of economic regeneration and overtures to working-class people were well received in these Rust Belt states.

Other battlefields:

North Carolina, Ohio, and Iowa all played important roles in Trump's triumph, reflecting changes in voter demographics and political alignments in these areas.

Reaction and Protest

Public and International Reactions

Domestic Reactions:

The election results elicited a wide spectrum of sentiments throughout the United States. Trump supporters praised what they saw as a historic and transformational triumph, while Clinton backers and others voiced astonishment, sadness, and anxiety about the country's future under Trump's administration.

"Not My President" Protests

Protests erupted in numerous major cities around the country in the days following the election, with the slogan "Not My President." Demonstrators opposed Trump's ideas, language, and the electoral college system as a whole. The protests highlighted the fundamental differences in American society and lasted several weeks following the election.

International Reactions

Global concerns:

Internationally, the victory of Donald Trump has caused anxiety and uncertainty among international leaders and citizens. Trump's campaign pledges, notably on trade, immigration, and foreign policy, have raised concerns about future adjustments in US global leadership and diplomatic ties.

Diplomatic outreach:

Following Trump's election, international leaders reached out to build early connections and grasp his administration's intentions. The global reaction was mixed, with some expressing cautious optimism and others voicing doubt and anxiety.

Transition of Power

Obama's role during the transition

Smooth Transition Traditions:

Despite their political disagreements, President Obama pledged to provide a peaceful and orderly handover of power to President-elect Trump. Both presidents stressed the necessity of maintaining governance and national security throughout the transition phase.

Meetings and briefings:

President Barack Obama and President-elect Donald Trump met at the White House and discussed critical policy areas, national security challenges, and presidential responsibilities. Obama supplied Trump with intelligence briefings and other tools to help with the transition.

Initial Actions of President-Elect Trump

Cabinet appointments:

Following his election, Donald Trump began putting together his government, picking key cabinet members and advisors. His decisions, which included contentious appointments and nominations, revealed his policy interests and attitude to governing.

Policy Signals:

Trump's early remarks and actions, including detailing his legislative agenda, issuing policy directives, and interfacing with Congress and foreign leaders, provide light on his administration's aims and governing style.

Public Statements and Twitter Use:

Trump continues to utilize Twitter to engage with the public and address policy concerns, provoking discussions and reactions both locally and globally. His unusual approach to communication established a model for presidential participation in the digital era.

To summarize, the aftermath of the 2016 presidential election was marked by a disparity between electoral college and popular vote results, significant reactions and protests, and the start of a power shift from President Obama to President-elect Trump. The election results revealed fundamental differences in American society, while domestically and international responses emphasized the outcome's global significance and ramifications for US domestic and foreign policy.

Chapter 10: Legacy and Impact.

Chapter 10: Legacy and Impact.

The 2016 presidential election made a lasting impression on American politics, culture, and future elections. This chapter investigates the political realignment that happened inside the Republican and Democratic parties, as well as the long-term implications for American politics and society.

Political realignment

Changes within the Republican Party

Populist Turn:

Donald Trump's win in the 2016 election signaled a substantial change in the Republican Party toward populism and nationalism. Trump's outsider status, anti-establishment rhetoric, and emphasis on subjects like immigration, trade, and economic nationalism transformed the party's platform and goals.

Division and realignment:

Trump's election and subsequent administration revealed serious fissures within the Republican Party between establishment elites and grassroots groups supportive of Trump's agenda. This internal conflict continues to impact party dynamics and primary elections.

Policy shifts:

Under Trump's leadership, the Republican Party shifted to policies that prioritized deregulation, tax reduction, conservative court selections, and a more forceful position on topics like immigration and national security.

Changes within the Democratic Party

Progressive Momentum:

Bernie Sanders' excellent performance in the Democratic primaries demonstrated the party's rising support for progressive objectives like as economic reform, expanded healthcare, and addressing income inequality.

Identity Politics & Diversity:

The 2016 election underlined the Democratic Party's commitment to diversity, inclusivity, and identity politics. Racial justice, LGBTQ+ rights, and women's rights were key components of the party's program and rhetoric.

Internal debate:

The Democratic Party was divided over its future orientation, with conflicts between progressive and moderate elements. These arguments continue to influence party strategy and policy views in future elections.

Long-Term Effects

Impact on American Politics and Society.

Polarization and division:

The 2016 election fueled political polarization and socioeconomic tensions in the United States. Debates concerning immigration, race relations, healthcare, and economic inequality became more inflamed, contributing to stalemate and party disagreement in Congress and the general public.

Media and Information Landscape:

The election demonstrated the impact of social media, "fake news," and misinformation efforts on public opinion and election results. These elements continue to influence the media environment, raising worries about the legitimacy of democratic processes.

Erosion of Trust:

After the 2016 election, trust in political institutions, media organizations, and government agencies deteriorated. Skepticism regarding electoral integrity, foreign influence, and the role of money in politics grew common among voters.

Influence on Future Elections

Campaign Strategy and Tactics:

The techniques and tactics used by candidates and parties during the 2016 election, such as digital marketing, data analytics, and tailored messaging, established precedents for future electoral campaigns. These technologies continue to evolve and influence electioneering techniques.

Election Security and Integrity:

The discoveries of foreign meddling and cybersecurity weaknesses in the 2016 election sparked attempts to improve election security, protect voter information, and reduce foreign influence in future elections.

Voter engagement and turnout:

The high stakes nature of the 2016 election, along with scandals and clear policy differences, enhanced voter involvement and turnout in future elections. Efforts to increase voter access and participation have become top concerns for election reform supporters.

To summarize, the 2016 presidential election has had a substantial and diverse influence on political dynamics, cultural trends, and electoral techniques in the United States. The election has hastened political realignment between the Republican and Democratic parties, increased polarization, and raised serious concerns about democratic norms and institutions. As America continues to deal with the fallout from 2016, the lessons gained and problems encountered will continue to affect the future of American politics and government.

Conclusion

Conclusion

The 2016 presidential campaign is seen as a watershed period in American political history, marked by tremendous drama, controversy, and major effects. As we reflect on this historic election, numerous major themes and lessons emerge, influencing our perception of its long-term history and influence on American culture and politics.

Reflections on the 2016 Campaign

Lessons Learned

The impact of populism and nationalism:

Donald Trump's triumph demonstrated the effectiveness of populist and nationalist appeals in American politics. His outsider status and direct communication approach appealed to those dissatisfied with mainstream politics and looking for change.

Role of Identity Politics:

Identity politics played an important role, with discussions about race, gender, and immigration impacting voter views and political agendas. Both parties dealt with concerns of inclusiveness, diversity, and representation.

Media and Information Influence:

The election demonstrated the power of social media, "fake news," and internet misinformation tactics to shape public opinion and political outcomes. This prompted questions about the credibility of information and media literacy.

Economic Discontent:

Economic worries, particularly among working-class voters in Rust Belt areas, fueled support for politicians who promised to revitalize manufacturing, renegotiate trade agreements, and address income inequality.

The 2016 Election's Long-Term Impact on American History

Political realignment:

The election caused a realignment between both main parties, with Republicans embracing populism and Democrats divided between progressive and moderate sections. This trend continues to influence party programs and election strategy.

Polarization and division:

The election deepened political polarization and cultural differences, fueling discussions over healthcare, immigration, racial justice, and the role of government. These differences continue to shape public discourse and policy discussions.

Election Security and Integrity:

Concerns about election security, foreign meddling, and voter suppression drove measures aimed at protecting democratic processes and increasing openness in elections.

Appendices

Timeline of Key Events

A complete chronological review of major events, debates, primaries, controversies, and electoral milestones from the beginning of the campaign until the inauguration.

Key Speeches and Quotes.

A collection of crucial speeches made by candidates, prominent supporters, and opponents during the campaign, showcasing critical events and language that resonated with voters.

Polling Data and Analysis

Comprehensive examination of polling data, including trends, techniques, and critical insights into voter preferences, changes, and prediction accuracy as Election Day approaches.

Further Reading and References

A curated selection of recommended reads, scholarly articles, books, and resources for further investigation into many facets of the 2016 presidential campaign, including its influence and historical context.

To summarize, the 2016 presidential election was more than just a fight between candidates; it reflected deep-seated social worries, political upheavals, and rising challenges to American democracy. As we continue to examine its impact and ramifications, the lessons from this historic election will influence our understanding of modern politics and inform future electoral methods and changes.

Outro

Outro

As we wrap up this voyage through the tumultuous and revolutionary 2016 presidential election, we are reminded that history is more than just a collection of events; it is a reflection of our common goals, struggles, and values. The campaign that transpired during those key months challenged our preconceptions, put our institutions to the test, and ultimately transformed the trajectory of American politics.

In investigating the dynamics of this historic election—from the rise of unusual candidates to seismic upheavals inside political parties—we dug into the complexity of democracy. We have tackled concerns of identity, ideology, and governance, which continue to reverberate in our national conversation and affect the political landscape.

However, despite the drama and controversy, the 2016 election has taught us valuable lessons. It has taught us about the strength of grassroots movements and the impact of social media on voter mobilization. It has emphasised the value of openness, honesty, and resilience in our election systems. It has also highlighted the need of civic involvement and educated citizenry in protecting our democratic institutions.

As we look ahead, may we take forth the lessons learned from this historic occasion. Let us strive for unity among variety, find common ground in the face of division, and maintain the ideals that unite us as a country. Let us be alert stewards of democracy, devoted to ensuring that every voice is heard, every vote counts, and every citizen has the opportunity to shape our country's future.

Thank you for joining me on my journey through the 2016 presidential campaign. May this book be a monument to American democracy's resiliency, as well as a spark for careful contemplation and meaningful conversation. Let us continue to create the next chapters of our country's history with bravery, compassion, and a firm commitment to a future worthy of our loftiest goals.

www.ingramcontent.com/pod-product-compliance
Lightning Source LLC
Chambersburg PA
CBHW070758250726
48662CB00004B/1872